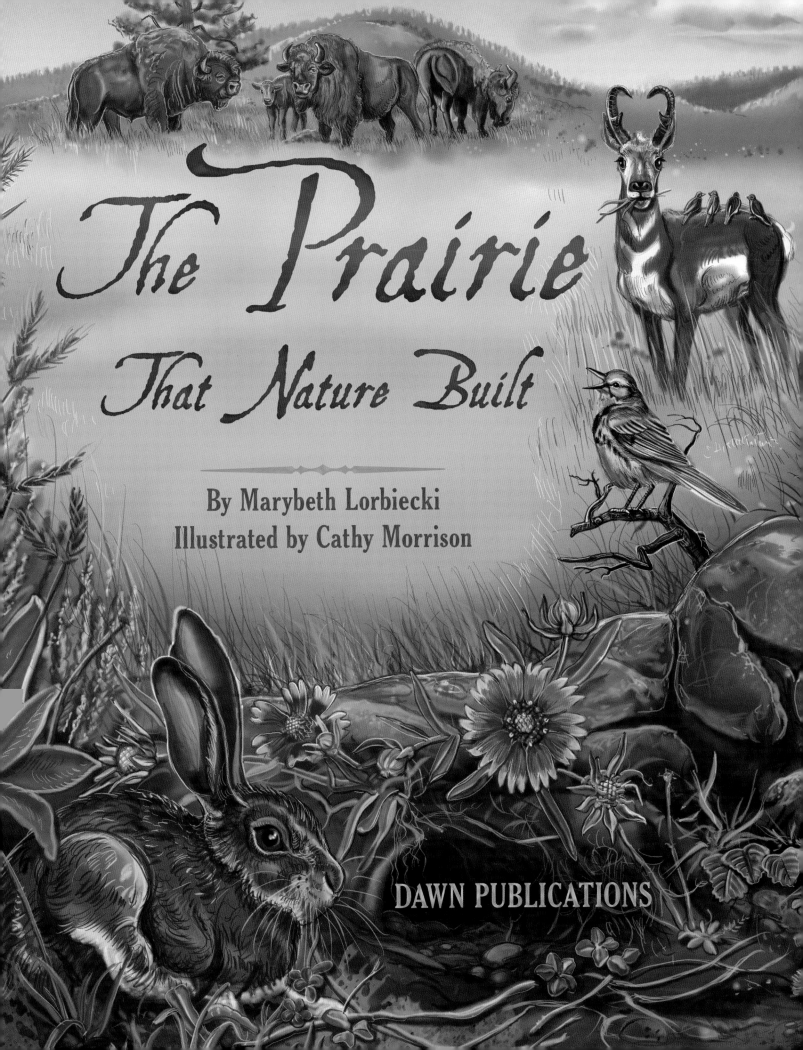

The Prairie
That Nature Built

By Marybeth Lorbiecki
Illustrated by Cathy Morrison

DAWN PUBLICATIONS

For Buck Malick, my prairie partner, and all our incredible comrades on the successful Western Wisconsin Prairie Project. — MbL

For Preston Barnes, an inspiring young man with lots of prairies to explore. — CM

Sincere thanks to both Kristen J. Hase, Natural Resource Program Manager at the Tallgrass Prairie National Preserve in Kansas, and Joshua Delger, Lead Wildlife Tech at Badlands National Park in South Dakota for their generous and courteous assistance.

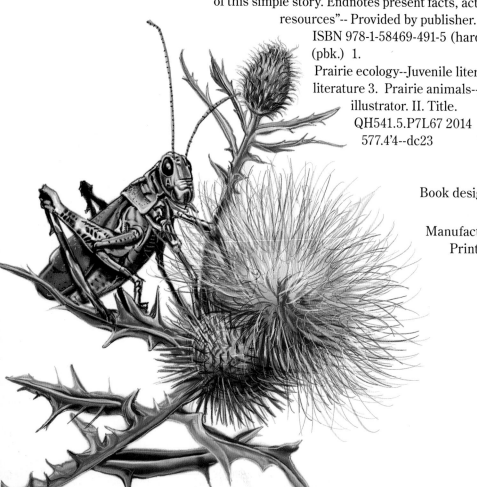

Library of Congress Cataloging-in-Publication Data
Lorbiecki, Marybeth.
  The prairie that nature built / by Marybeth Lorbiecki ; illustrated by Cathy Morrison.
    pages cm
  Summary: "Nature on the prairie, including both wildlife and wildfire, is a rich and closely knit ecosystem, as reflected in the interlocking verses of this simple story. Endnotes present facts, activities, related games, and resources"-- Provided by publisher.
    ISBN 978-1-58469-491-5 (hardback) -- ISBN 978-1-58469-492-2 (pbk.) 1.
  Prairie ecology--Juvenile literature. 2. Grassland ecology--Juvenile literature 3. Prairie animals--Juvenile literature. I. Morrison, Cathy, illustrator. II. Title.
    QH541.5.P7L67 2014
    577.4'4--dc23
                                                  2013049138

Book design and computer production by Patty Arnold,
Menagerie Design & Publishing

Manufactured by Regent Publishing Services, Hong Kong
Printed May, 2014, in ShenZhen, Guangdong, China

10 9 8 7 6 5 4 3 2 1
First Edition

DAWN PUBLICATIONS
12402 Bitney Springs Road
Nevada City, CA 95959
530-274-7775
nature@dawnpub.com

This is the prairie that nature built.

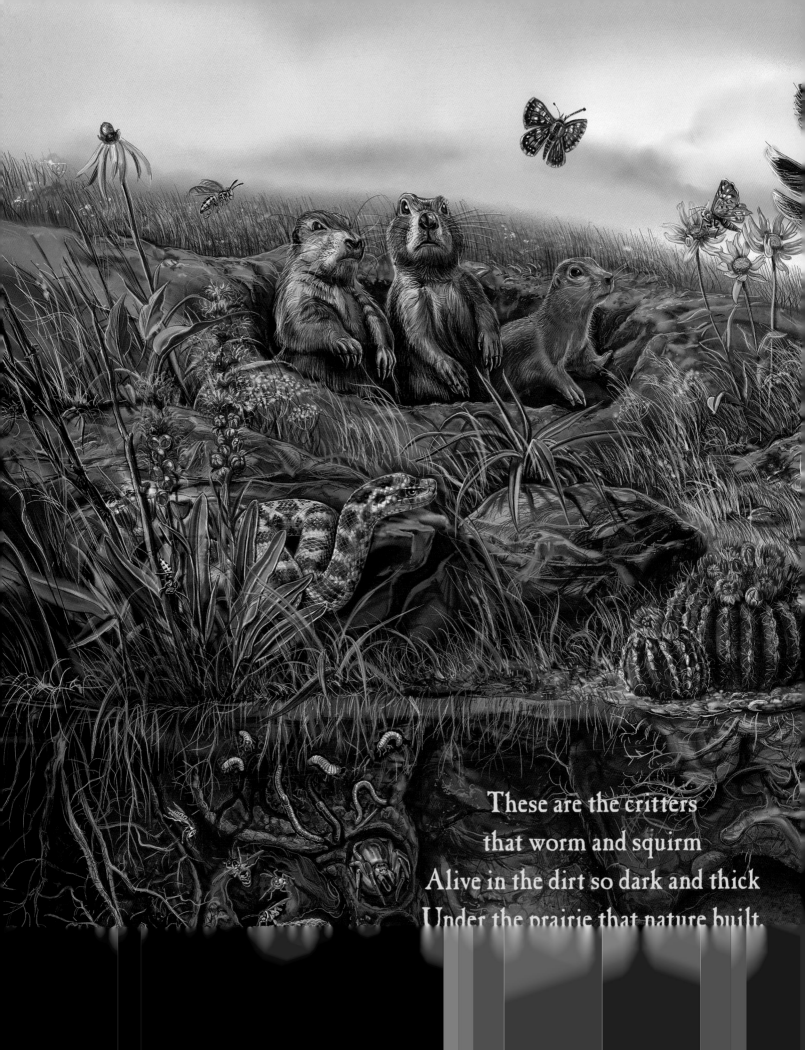

These are the critters
that worm and squirm
Alive in the dirt so dark and thick
Under the prairie that nature built.

Some of these critters squirm so small
Without a glass, you can't see them all.
But they are big eaters
and builders too,
Making good earth from animal poo.

These are the diggers, with tunnels so steep,
Making soft burrows where prairie pups sleep,
Alongside the critters that worm and squirm
Alive in the dirt so dark and thick
Under the prairie that nature built.
Prairie dogs dig tunnels galore—
Lucky for owls, snakes,
ferrets, and more!

These are the roots that plunge so deep,
Long and strong, holding water to keep,
Down past the burrows where prairie pups sleep,
Alongside the critters that worm and squirm
Alive in the dirt so dark and thick
Under the prairie that nature built.
Such long, strong roots can save the day
When rain you want still stays away.

These are the plants that shoot so high,
Seeking food from above, the sunlit sky,
Up from the roots that plunge so deep,
Down past the burrows where prairie pups sleep.
Alongside the critters that worm and squirm
Alive in the dirt so dark and thick
Under the prairie that nature built.
The sky-reaching plants turn toward the sun
Following the path of its east-to-west run.

These are the insects so fragile and shy
That buzzing and whirring bring pollen by
To all the plants that shoot for the sky,
Up from the roots that plunge so deep,
Down past the burrows where prairie pups sleep,
Alongside the critters that worm and squirm
Alive in the dirt so dark and thick
Under the prairie that nature built.
Some of the butterflies whir from so far,
They've traveled from Mexico — without a car!

These are the birds that sing and fly,
Chomping the insects that bring pollen by
To all the plants that shoot for the sky,
Up from the roots that plunge so deep.
Some high-soaring birds when looking to eat
Find prairie dog meat a tasty treat.

These are the grazers munching so mild
On grasses and flowers stomped and piled,
Under the birds that sing and fly,
Chomping the insects that bring pollen by
To all the plants that shoot for the sky,
Up from the roots that plunge so deep,
Down past the burrows where prairie pups sleep,
Alongside the critters that worm and squirm
Alive in the dirt so dark and thick
Under the prairie that nature built.
The four-hoofed grazers like to mosey in herds,
And calmly chew grasses while groomed by birds.

These are the hunters, so skillful and wild,
Preparing to pounce on the grazers so mild,
Under dark clouds where thunder booms.
For all in the prairie, danger looms!

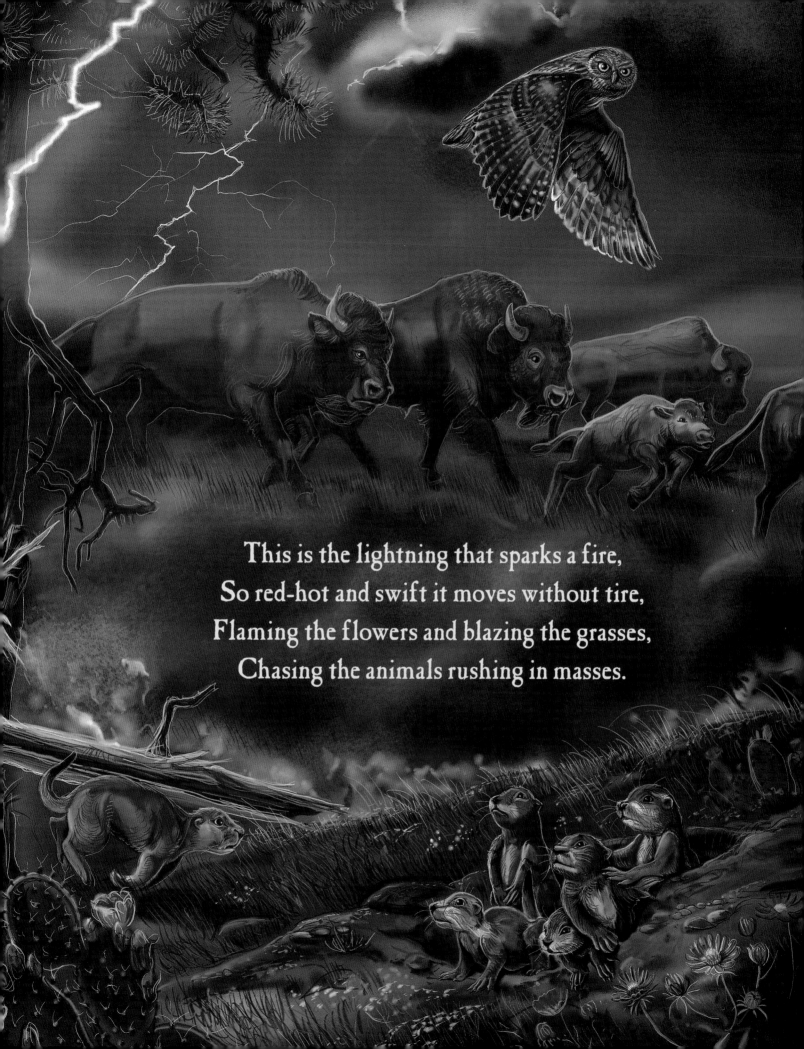

This is the lightning that sparks a fire,
So red-hot and swift it moves without tire,
Flaming the flowers and blazing the grasses,
Chasing the animals rushing in masses.

This is the rain that splatters the ground,
And quenches the fire that blazed all around.

Months later—surprise!
Quite out of the blue,
Out pop green stalks
All bright and brand new,
Painting the ashes with color and dew.
The blazing fire that blackened the reeds
Fed the ground and
Burst out seeds.

This is the one, when taking a walk,
Found a bloom upon a green stalk,
Who saw the lightning
And felt the rain
That killed the fire
And calmed the plain,
Who heard the birds
Singing so high
And smelled the flowers
Where insects flit by,
And spotted the doggies
Ducking to hide
In tunnels so steep,
Plunging past roots,
Stretching so deep,
Alongside the critters
That worm and squirm
Alive in the dirt
So dark and thick
Under the prairie that nature built.

This is the prairie that grows so free.
And this is the kid that loves it — me!

A Prairie Primer

Over one fourth of the earth's land was once covered with grasslands. These grassy plains filled with life are called by different names around the world. In North America grasslands are called *prairies*. In Africa, where lions stalk zebra, giraffe, elephants, and gazelle, grasslands dotted with a few trees are called *savannas*. In Eastern Europe and Asia they are called *steppes*, and in South America they are called *pampas*, *llano*, or *cerrados*. Australians call grasslands *rangelands*.

The prairies of North America covered much of the Great Plains, from east of the Mississippi River to the Rocky Mountains. They stretched as far as any eye could see–an ocean of grasses! The grasses in the wetter parts of the Great Plains would grow really tall–over six feet high. A person on horseback could ride through and hardly be seen. In the dry parts of the West and Southwest, the grasses were far shorter, usually under one foot high. Between the tall-grass and short-grass prairies would be mixed-grass prairies, with both short and tall grasses and flowers. The type of prairie depends upon the amount of rainfall the plants receive.

Prairie wetlands, called *prairie potholes*, can be found in northern U.S. and southern Canada. They attract grazers and birds. These marshy potholes are so important for ducks that they've been called "North America's duck factories." These grassy ponds provide habitat for pintail ducks, green-winged teal, shovelers, canvasbacks, and many more. Egrets and herons, turtles, frogs, and muskrats love them too. As we lose prairies and prairie potholes, we lose prairie birds and waterfowl. Prairie birds are declining faster than all other kinds of North American birds.

Prairie plants have deep, deep roots so they can suck up water from underground reserves and hold it. Some tall-grasses and plants have roots deeper than twenty feet – equal to the height of a two-story building. Prairie fires burn off dead grass and flowers, making room for new plants to grow, but the flames don't kill the plants. Their roots are protected in the earth. The fires turn the dead leaves and stalks into ashes that help fertilize the soil.

Bison (also called buffalo), pronghorn antelope, wolves, grizzlies and even cougars used to live in the prairies. Many Plains Indian tribes, such as the Lakota Sioux, hunted the buffalo and ducks, and harvested wild rice. They cut sweetgrass stalks and dug up roots for food.

An organization in Kansas called **The Land Institute** is experimenting with harvesting prairie grasses for food. They grind the grains to make breads and muffins and other foods. Maybe someday you'll be eating prairie bread.

When immigrant farmers came to the prairies, there weren't trees with which to build houses. So they cut up the earth into bricks to make sod houses. These immigrants were called *sodbusters*. Today some people are planting "prairies" on rooftops! Chicago's City Hall, whose roof is eleven stories high, has a prairie on it —with its own beehives, but no bison or prairie dogs. There are more than 600 "green roofs" in Chicago alone. Even in New York City, prairie plants now grow on the "high line," an abandoned railroad track bed built above city streets. These above-ground prairies help the city stay alive with birds and butterflies and people. They remind us how even more beautiful, wild, and full of wildlife our natural prairies are, so we keep our on-the-ground prairies alive and well—and replant them wherever we can.

Prairies are crucial habitats for the health of the planet. They absorb great amounts of carbon and help slow climate change. Sadly, only four percent of North America's original grasslands still exist. Most have been cut up for farming and building. Many Native American Indian nations have been working hard to bring back the prairies and the buffalo on their lands. National and state parks and nature centers are working to preserve prairies, too. If you visit these lively places, see for yourself how many species you can count.

Soil Partners

In the earth, bacteria and other micro-organisms live together to help make the soil healthy. Worms, insects, spiders, ants, and other small creatures crawl through, making air holes. These air holes keep the soil from baking into a brick. When it rains, the water flows through these small holes. These "partners" help make the soil fertile for farming. However, pesticides and other chemicals kill many species that live in the soil and make it so fertile and alive.

Burrowers

Mice, moles, and prairie dogs tunnel in the prairie earth. Burrowing owls dig their own homes or use the abandoned rooms of the prairie dogs. Ferrets and snakes use the prairie dog tunnels too.

Scavengers

Scavengers are those useful creatures who eat animal poop and dead animals. Some are insects, like dung beetles, while others are worms, centipedes, and millipedes. Birds that scavenge include crows, ravens, and magpies.

Grasses and Flowers

Prairies have a mix of so many different grasses and flowers that something is blooming through every week of the spring, summer, and fall. Winter brings a rest for the soil and the perennial plants that store their food in their roots.

Pollinators

Flitting about from flower to flower are bees, wasps, beetles, flies, and butterflies. They carry pollen from plant to plant, which allows the plants to make seeds.

Seedeaters

Mice and many birds love plant seeds. Thistle seed are a favorite of goldfinches. Bluebirds, bobolinks and bobwhites, meadowlarks and field sparrows, pheasants and prairie chickens feast on a buffet of so many different seeds. When seeds get caught in an animal's fur or feathers, they get scattered, to be planted in new locations. Seeds also get pooped out as natural fertilizer for the prairie.

Grazers

Bison and antelope travel in herds over the grassy plains. When they are hunted by wolves or cougars, they keep moving. They churn up the soil with their hooves, which encourages seeds to sprout, and they leave poop behind which becomes food for the soil. This is known as the "stomp and poop" method that helps a prairie grow. However, if there are no predators to keep them moving, the grazer's hooves grind up the grasslands, killing the plants. Without plants to hold it down, the soil blows or washes away. Herds of cattle and sheep can be made to act like the natural grazers by moving them every day to two. Smaller animals, like prairie dogs, are also grazers, eating the plants, and so are grasshoppers.

Predators

Animals that eat others—*predators*—come in all sizes. The wolf spider stalks its prey of insects while packs of gray wolves stalk herds of pronghorn. Coyotes tend to be loners, snatching a mouse or prairie dog whenever they can. Red-tailed hawks and golden eagles soar overhead, waiting to dive on an unsuspecting rabbit or prairie dog. These natural predators help keep animal populations healthy by keeping them from getting too numerous to have enough food. They also keep them moving to new grasses so they don't eat too much in one area. Predators eat the sick, old, young, or weak members. Most prairie animals have to watch out for hunting humans, too.

Prairie Fun

Name them! How many different species you can find in the illustrations in this book? Look for these and other:

Plants: prairie larkspur, butterfly milkweed, flowering cactus, blazing star, purple coneflower, black-eyed Susans, blanket flower, goldenrod

Insects and arachnids: pill bugs, wolf spider, wasps, honey bee, monarch butterfly, swallowtail butterfly, regal fritillary butterfly, dung beetles

Birds: bluebird, meadowlark, red-tailed hawks, prairie chicken, burrowing owls

Reptiles: bull snake, garter snake, ornate box turtle

Mammals: deer mouse, prairie dogs, bison, ferrets, pronghorn antelope, coyotes, wolves, black-tailed jackrabbit

A key to all species illustrated in the book is available at www.dawnpub.com under the "Activities" tab.

Count them! Visit a prairie near you and see how many species you can find. Use the book and field guides to help you name them. Challenge yourself to find one from each of the five categories above and five plants of different colors.

Dinners and diners! Play a tag game of prairie dinners and diners by choosing a few kids to be a prairie predator, such as a wolf. All of the other players are prey, such as antelopes. Designate a safe spot, home base, and at a signal have all of the antelopes try to make it to home base without being tagged by the wolves. If they are only tagged by one wolf, they are only wounded.

Mind the monarchs! Raise and tag monarch butterflies as part of the Journey North Butterfly project, http://www.learner.org/jnorth/monarch/index.html, or Monarch Watch, http://www.monarchwatch.org/. You can learn about the monarchs and their migrations, and even link up with kids in Mexico.

Great Prairie Parks to Visit There are many wonderful prairie parks throughout the Midwest. An excellent map and prairie information can be found at http://www.eng.iastate.edu/explorer/Old%20web/topics/prairies/where.htm Find prairies in Canada, including the Canadian Grasslands National Park and Prince Albert National Park in Saskatchewan.

Great Prairie Organizations and Websites

Alberta Prairie Conservation Forum: www.albertapcf.org

Camp Silos (from Silos and Smokestacks Nat. Heritage Center: www.campsilos.org/mod1/index.shtml

Grand Prairie Friends (in east-central Illinois): grandprairiefriends.org

Iowa Prairie Network: www.iowaprairienetwork.org

Konza Prairie: keep.konza.ksu.edu

Missouri Prairie Foundation: www.moprairie.org

NWF Rocky Mountains and Prairies: www.nwf.org/Rocky-Mountains-and-Prairies.aspx

Prairie Enthusiasts (Upper Midwest): www.theprairieenthusiasts.org

Saskatchewan Prairie Conservation Action Plan: www.pcap-sk.org

For to Explore—Prairies: www.42explore.com/prairie.htm

Wild Ones—Native Plants, Native Landscapes, Healing the Earth One Yard at a Time: www.wildones.org

TED Talk by Allan Savory about moving herds of grazers to recover grasslands that have been turning to desert. Savory is referring to former grasslands that are losing soil and grasses, not to natural deserts, which are different, vibrant ecosystems. www.ted.com

Great Prairie Books

America's Prairies and Grasslands: A Guide to the Plants and Animals by Marianne D. Wallace (Fulcrum Press, 2001)

One Day in the Prairie by Jean Craighead George (Trophy Book, 1996)

Prairie Dogs by Marybeth Lorbiecki (Northword-Cooper Square Publishing, 2004)

Prairies by Dorothy Hinshaw Patent (Holiday House, 1996)

A Tallgrass Prairie Alphabet by Claudia McGehee (University of Iowa Press, 2004)

Marybeth Lorbiecki grew up in St. Cloud, Minnesota, near a prairie, before she knew it was called a prairie. Instead it was simply her favorite place for exploring and hiding amid the tall grasses. She would always be spotted by meadowlarks, who saluted her with song.

That prairie was built over with homes, and she no longer found her friends the larks there any more. When Marybeth moved to Hudson, Wisconsin, she became part of a group that taught the community about the amazing prairie that nature built. She brought her daughters and son to wander through the prairie grasses. Together they helped preserve prairies nearby so the meadowlarks would have a place to nest and sing. She's written more than twenty-five books for kids, many of them about the places, plants, and animals she loves, including the prairie dog!

Cathy Morrison is an award-winning illustrator who lives on a shortgrass prairie in Colorado, at the western edge of the Great Plains in view of the Rocky Mountain National Forest. She watches the grasses, the animals and their burrows, as well as floods and fire—all close up and personal. She began her career in animation and graphic design, but discovered her passion for children's book illustration while raising her two children. After several years illustrating with traditional media, she now works digitally, which helps the publisher adapt the art into interactive book apps. This is Cathy's first book for Dawn Publications.

Some of Dawn's Books, Ebooks, and Interactive Book Apps

Dawn's books are also available as ebooks, plus some are also interactive book apps.

The Prairie that Nature Built — This book also has an **app**, in which the diggers dig, the birds, fly, and the grazers munch—and much more—when you touch them.

The Mouse and the Meadow — Experience the vibrant and sometimes dangerous nature of meadow life from a mouse's eye-view. In the **book app**, touch the characters and see them move! This book also has a free Pop-Up App.

The Swamp Where Gator Hides — Look for gator hiding in the algae, and learn about the turtle, vole, bobcat, duck, sunfish, and other animals that are home there. In the **book app**, help them escape gator's fast-approaching jaws!

Noisy Frog Sing-Along — See the many kinds of frogs that make all kinds of sounds — without ever opening their mouths! In the **book app**, watch their bulgy throat pouches expand, then play the game by matching their sounds (and sound waves) with each kind of frog.

Noisy Bug Sing-Along — An amazing concert of sounds is happening every day, made by insects that have no vocal chords! In the **book app**, see how they move different body parts to make sounds, then play the matching game.

Over in the Ocean — Coral reefs are teeming with colorful mamas and babies. You can count and sing along. In the **book app**, little fingers can make the octopus squirt, and the pufferfish puff! Then play the counting game challenge to find all 55 babies hiding in the coral reef.

Over in the Jungle — Count, clap, and sing among enchanting rainforest animals and their babies. In the **book app**, watch the ocelots pounce, parrots squawk, and boas squeeze – and then find all the babies hiding in the jungle floor and canopy.

Dandelion Seed's Big Dream — This "weed" seed flies with beauty, survives storms, endures darkness, never gives up. It is one of nature's greatest success stories that makes the world a brighter place.

In the Trees, Honey Bees — Truly remarkable and valuable creatures live inside a tree. We are treated to an inside-the-hive view of a wild colony, along with solid information.

Dawn Publications is dedicated to inspiring in children a deeper understanding and appreciation for all life on Earth. You can browse through our titles, download resources for teachers, and order at www.dawnpub.com or call 800-545-7475.